Copyright © 2020 by Henry Hooks

All rights reserved. This book or any portion thereof may not be reproduced or used in any manner whatsoever without the express written permission of the publisher. Please send such requests to: *acmpublish@gmail.com*

ISBN: 978-1-7332919-3-4

Book cover designed by: Angela Miles

Published by: A&C Marketplace Publishing LLP in the United States of America

TABLE OF CONTENT		PAGE
Introduction		6
Spiritual Acronymic Bible Study Index		8
The Lord Comforts Me: A Poetic Psalms 23 Praise		22
Bible Study 1	Our Master	23
Bible Study 2	His Message	31
Bible Study 3	His Ministry	39
Bible Study 4	His Mandate	47
Bible Study 5	Our Ministry	55
Bible Study 6	Our Maturation	63
Bible Study 7	Our Milestone	71
Bible Study 8	His Promises Manifested	79
Psalms 34	Poetic Concordance	87
Bible Study 9	Recessed In Dimness	90
Bible Study 10	Residing In Darkness	97
Bible Study 11	Rendered In Desolation	104
Psalms 91	Poetic Concordance	111

Introduction

The SOS Spiritual Acronymic Dictionary and Bible Study Guide was written to benefit all of God's chosen people, no matter where one's current place is in the body of Christ.

The anchoring focus is aimed at furthering any believer's personal and self compelling growth in the righteousness of our Lord and Savior Jesus Christ through prayerfully assembled spiritual acronyms and Bible study content that inspires, entertains, educates, and edifies (IEEE).

The IEEE Spiritual Mindset

IEEE (Inspire, Entertain, Educate, Edify) is the acronym which best represents the spiritual mindset that the Lord God imparted unto me for the purpose of effectively transitioning my primary focus onto Him and His word, so that I thereafter could prayerfully impart the same focus onto the authoring of this book.

The Salvation Over Sin (SOS) Concept

Salvation over Sin (SOS) is equal in meaning to the expressions "Supernatural over Natural" and "Spirit over Flesh".

We know that victory in salvation does not come by any works of the flesh, and thus it is not by any natural or physical means. So we thereby know that God created and instituted salvation to be a harvest that is reaped from the blood of the sacrificial Lamb of God (our Lord and Savior Jesus Christ) by means of the invincible resurrection power of the Holy Spirit.

Through the namesake of our Lord and Savior Jesus Christ, salvation is a victory that is initially sowed into God's supernatural realm by way of a Christian believer's faith in God. The harvest of salvation is consequentially manifested into the natural realm by the continuance of a Christian believer's faith in God through the tests and trials of life.

Thus the only passageway into God's supernatural realm from the natural realm is through our Lord and Savior Jesus Christ. He is the way, the truth, and the light.

Salvation is transformative, consumptive and intimate. It ignites a personal relationship between a Christian believer and our Lord and Savior Jesus Christ and culminates, by way of faith and perseverance, into blessedly assured sainthood, everlasting fellowship with our Almighty God, and eternal life with Him in heaven.

SPIRITUAL ACRONYMIC BIBLE STUDY INDEX

ADVOCATES   Bible Study 5

Anyone Dedicated to Voluntary Outreaches of Care that Administer via Testimony, Education, and Supplementation

ANGEL   Bible Study 1

Abiding Noble Guardian of Eternal Life

ANOINTING   Bible Study 6

Ascribed Noteworthy Obedience that Inspires Nature's Transcendence via Intercession Necessitated by God

ARMOR   Bible Study 5

Adeptness at Repelling the Malevolent Opponents of Righteousness

BEAUTY   Bible Study 8

Bountifully Exquisite Attributes Unveiling a Treasure in You

BELIEF   Bible Study 2

Bond Empowered by the Lord that is Inspirationally Established in Faith

BLESSED   Bible Study 3

Believers of the Lord Extensively Supplemented and Secure Every Day

BLESSING   Bible Study 3

Bountifulness of the Lord Extended Significantly to the Saved, via Intercession Necessitated by God

BLOOD   Bible Study 1

Banner of Love Outstretched Over Destiny

BODY   Bible Study 4

Biological Offspring Devoted to Yearning

CALM   Bible Study 3

Comfort Attained in the Lord's Mercy

CARE   Bible Study 5

Compassionate Attention to Rightful Entitlements

CHURCH   Bible Study 5

Consecrated Home of the Uplifted Righteous in Christ, the Head

COMFORT   Bible Study 3

Confidence Overflowing Majestically in Faith and Operating Relentlessly in Trust

CONCERN   Bible Study 5

Cautious Overflow of Nervousness, Concentrated on Eliminating or Remediating Needs

CONFIDENCE   Bible Study 6

Conducting Obligations Noteworthily with Fulfillment that Illustrates Dedication, Enthusiasm, Nobleness, and Christian Empowerment

CROSS   Bible Study 1

Cost Required to Obliterate Sin and Suffering

DIGNITY   Bible Study 5

Dominion of Integrity, Gallantly Navigating Interpersonal Treatment in You

DISCIPLE   Bible Study 5

Dedicated Individual Serving Christians and Inspiring People to Love Everyone

DREAMS   **Bible Study 7**

Destiny's Revelations Entailed in Analyzable Memories as Signs

FAITH   **Bible Study 2**

Fostering the Anointing Invincibly via Trust and Hope

FAMILY   **Bible Study 2**

Fellowship of Abiding Members Interactively Loving You

FAVOR   **Bible Study 7**

Faithfulness Awarded Vividly Onto the Righteous

FAVORED   **Bible Study 7**

Faithfulness Awarded Vividly Onto the Righteous Every Day

FORGIVE   **Bible Study 6**

Forgetting and Omission of Retribution on Grievances, and Issuing Vengeance Exoneration

FREE   **Bible Study 3**

Fetters Removed and Enemies Eliminated

FREEDOM   **Bible Study 3**

Fetters Removed and Enemies Entirely Destroyed Omnisciently by the Messiah

FRIEND   **Bible Study 2**

Faithful Relationship Inspirationally Established with Notable Dignity

GIFT   **Bible Study 6**

Gratifying Investment Favorably Transacted

GIVE   **Bible Study 6**

Gratify with Investments Voluntarily Extended

GLORIFIED Bible Study 1

God's Lovingkindness and Omnipotence Reigning, and Invincibly Facilitating the Interdependent Events of Destiny

GLORY Bible Study 3

God's Love Overflowing and Rising in You

GOOD Bible Study 5

God's Omniscience Obediently Demonstrated

GRACE Bible Study 2

Godly Redemption Assured via Christ's Empathy

HALLOWED Bible Study 1

Held Above the Land of the Living Omnipotently With Everlasting Dedication

HARVEST Bible Study 8

Hearty Abundance Received Via Excessive Seed Transformation

HEALED Bible Study 6

Having Elements of Affliction Lastingly and Evidentially Defeated

HEALING Bible Study 6

Help to Eliminate Afflictions Lastingly by the Intercession and Namesake of God

HEART Bible Study 4

Habitual Emotions that Administer to Relationships and Trust

HEAVEN Bible Study 1

Home Eternally to the Acclaimed and Vindicated Exemplifiers of Nobility

HELP   Bible Study 2

Humbly Extending Love and Provisions

HOLINESS   Bible Study 1

Hallelujahs Outpouring unto the Lamb and Intense Noble Enthusiasm Saturating the Sanctuary

HONEST   Bible Study 7

Holding Onto Nobility and Earnestness via the Sacred Truth

HOPE   Bible Study 2

Help Orchestrated in Prayer and Evangelism

HUMBLE   Bible Study 2

Having an Unselfish Mind Bound by a Lighthearted Ego

JOY   Bible Study 3

Jubilation of Overwhelming Yield

JUDGEMENT   Bible Study 4

Jesus's Uncompromisable Decisions on Good and Evil to Mandate the Eternal Nonproliferation of Transgressions

JUSTICE   Bible Study 4

Judgement Upon Sin Theocratically Imposed and Conclusively Enforced

KIND   Bible Study 5

Keen Interpersonal Niceness Displayed

KNOWLEDGE   Bible Study 7

Keenness in the Necessity of Obedience to the Word of the Lord and Enthusiastic Devotion to Godly Education

LAW   **Bible Study 4**
Legitimized Article of the Word

LIFE   **Bible Study 2**
Love Incarnated and Forwardly Evolving

LIGHT   **Bible Study 1**
Luminous Intimacy of God's Holy Trinity

LOVE   **Bible Study 1**
Life Overjoyed and Victorious Everyday

MERCY   **Bible Study 3**
Method of Extending the Righteousness of Christ to You

MIND   **Bible Study 4**
Map to the Imagination and Navigator to Decisions

MIRACLE   **Bible Study 8**
Monumental and Incredible Result of the Anointing and Consequence of the Lord's Exuberance

MORALS   **Bible Study 7**
Maturated Obligations to Ritually Accepted Laws and Standards

NEEDS   **Bible Study 6**
Notable Elements Essential to Daily Survival

NEIGHBOR   **Bible Study 2**
Nearby Engaging Individual with a Good Heart that Befriends with an Orderly Rapport

NOBLE   **Bible Study 8**
Noteworthy Obedient Beneficiary of Life Everlasting

OBEDIENCE   Bible Study 6

Obligations to the Biblical Execution of Duties that are Integrally Evident of Noteworthy Christian Education

PATIENCE   Bible Study 6

Poised Awaiting of Time to Inspirationally Empower Needs to Come into Existence

PEACE   Bible Study 3

Pleasingly and Enthusiastically Anchored in Christ Evermore

PERSEVERANCE   Bible Study 7

Patience Everyday to Remain Strong, Earnest, and Vigilant in Events that Relentlessly Attempt to Neutralize Christian Empowerment

PRAISE   Bible Study 5

Providence Robustly Acclaimed in Inspirational Singing and Exhortation

PRAYERS   Bible Study 5

Petitions of the Righteous that Always Yield Everything Requested in Surplus

PROMISE   Bible Study 8

Provisions of Righteousness Obligated to be Manifested Insurmountably to Salvation's Elite

PURE   Bible Study 1

Perfected and Upstanding Righteous Existence

REDEEMED   Bible Study 8

Released from the Entanglements of Darkness and Evolving Everyday to a Mightily Enriched Destiny

REPENT   Bible Study 4

Regretting Earnestly Previous Events of Negativity and Transgression

RIGHT   Bible Study 6

Rewarded Intercession that Garnishes the Hallowed Truth

RIGHTEOUS   Bible Study 8

Renowned Individuals that Guard the Hallowed Truth and Exhibit Obedience Unto Sanctification

SACRED   Bible Study 1

Sanctified Article, Cherished Ritually and Established in Declaration

SACRIFICE   Bible Study 7

Surrendering All to Creditably Reflect Intense Faith Invested in Christ Eternally

SAFE   Bible Study 3

Secured Against the Forces of Evil

SAINTS   Bible Study 8

Salvation's Anointed and Integrated Nobles of a Theocratic Society

SALVATION   Bible Study 2

Spiritual Alignment to the Lord's Virtues that Admonish Transgressions and Inspire Obedience unto Nobility

SAVED   Bible Study 3

Securely Anchored to the Vine Each Day

SEED   Bible Study 6

Succeeding Evolutionary Element of Destiny

SHEPHERD   Bible Study 8

Savior's Hands Eternally Placed to Hold Everyone that is Redeemed and Delivered

SINCERE   Bible Study 7

Saturated Internally in Noticeable Christian Ethics and Righteous to Everyone

SOUL   Bible Study 4

Sacred Objectives of an Unbridled Life

SPIRIT   Bible Study 1

Sanctuary of Providence and Invulnerability Resurrected to Institute Theocracy

THANKS   Bible Study 5

Thoughtful Heralded Appreciation Noted for Kindness and Sacrifice

TRUST   Bible Study 2

Total Reliance Uploaded onto the Savior Timelessly

TRUTH   Bible Study 4

Theocratic Revelations that Unmask the Transgressions of Humanity

VALUE   Bible Study 7

Vetted Assertion that is Lasting, Undeniable, and Essential

VIRTUES   Bible Study 8

Vital Instructions on Righteousness Taught to Unify, Edify, and Sanctify

VISION   Bible Study 7

Vivid Introspective Spiritual Intercession that is Observed Noteworthily

VOWS   Bible Study 4

Voiced Obligations Willfully Stated

WILL   Bible Study 4

Worthy Intercessory Laws of the Lord

WISDOM   Bible Study 7

Willing Indoctrination of Scriptural Dominance Over the Mind

WORD   Bible Study 4

Wholehearted Obedience to Righteousness Defined

WORSHIP   Bible Study 8

Wholehearted Overflow of Reverence that Saturates Heaven and Invigorates Praises

---

ADULTERER   Bible Study 10

Anyone that Depicts Unfaithfulness by Lustfully Transgressing in an Extramarital Relationship and Evading the Repercussions

ADVERSARY   Bible Study 11

Anyone with Demonic Values that is Entrenched on Rejecting Salvation's Atonement and Redemptive Yearnings

ANGER   Bible Study 9

Animosity Noticeably Garnered and Expressed in a Rampage

BIGOTRY   Bible Study 10

Belligerence and Insults Guided at Outsiders of the Tribal Rudiments in You

BONDAGE Bible Study 9

Burdened, Oppressed, and Needlessly Defenseless Against the Gates of Evil

CURSE Bible Study 11

Conduct of Unrighteousness Resulting in Suffering and Exclusion

CURSED Bible Study 11

Conduct of Unrighteousness Resulting in Suffering and Eternal Damnation

DAMNATION Bible Study 11

Desolation Afflicted Meticulously upon the Nefarious Adversaries that Trust in Iniquity and Oppose the Noble

DEMON Bible Study 11

Devious Entity Missioned to Oppress the Nations

DEVIL Bible Study 11

Devious Entity with Vile Intentions Lurking

ENVIOUS Bible Study 10

Entrenched Nonsensically on the Valuables and Idiosyncrasies of Others, with Undermining Scorn

EVIL Bible Study 9

Events of Vileness, Idolatry, and Lustfulness

FILTHINESS Bible Study 11

Fostering of Intercommunicative Lewdness, Treatment of Hygiene Impairments with Neglect, and Eluding of Stench in the Soul

GREED Bible Study 10

Gathering and Retaining of Everything Essential Demonically

GUILT   Bible Study 10

Grief from Unrepentant Iniquity, Levying Torment

HATE   Bible Study 11

Hellish Anger and the Terror of Evildoers

HELL   Bible Study 11

Horrific Eradication Levied upon the Lawless

HYPOCRISY   Bible Study 10

Holding onto Yokes of Pretense that Obnoxiously Convey Religious Imitations of Salvation and its Yearnings

LAWLESSNESS   Bible Study 11

Legitimized Articles of the Word Loomingly Excluded in the Soul of a Sinner, Necessitating Either Salvation or Suffering

LEWDNESS   Bible Study 10

Lingering Elements of Wickedness Dispatching Nefariousness to Entrap the Soul of a Sinner

LIAR   Bible Study 9

Lawless Individual that Attacks Righteousness

LIES   Bible Study 9

Lawless Inferences of Evil Sources

LUST   Bible Study 10

Lewd Unrighteous Seeds of Transgression

OPPRESSION   Bible Study 10

Outward Pressures on People or Republics to Extort Submission to Strongholds and Impositions, with Opposition Noneffective

SAD   **Bible Study 9**

Sorrowful, Anguished, and/or Depressed

SELFISH   **Bible Study 10**

Strivings of an Egocentric Life that Foster Indecency and Scorn in the Heart

SIN   **Bible Study 9**

Subversive Infestation of Nature

STUBBORNNESS   **Bible Study 9**

Selfish Tenacity in Utilizing a Bolstered Bogus Opposition to Righteousness Naively to Nonsensically Elude Submission to Salvation

SUFFERING   **Bible Study 9**

Seeds of Unrighteousness that Form the Fruits of Eventual Retribution, Irrevocably Necessitated by Guilt

TROUBLE   **Bible Study 9**

Temporary Repercussions of Outbreaking Unrighteousness that Burden Life's Endeavors

                                                  END OF INDEX

THE LORD COMFORTS ME
A POETIC PSALMS 23 PRAISE

The Lord is my shepherd, and He is my Jehovah-Jirah.
I shall never want for anything for He shall always be my provider.

He makes me to lie down upon the most greenness and restful of
pastures. I awaken renewed and filled with
His heavenly joy and laughter.

He leads me quietly beside the calming, refreshingly still waters.
This the Lords does to instill peace inside all of His sons and daughters.

What is most amazing of all to me is how the Lord restores my soul.
For He does this for all of His saints no matter how young or old.

The Lord also leads me down the right path for the sake of His Holy
name. You see the steps of the righteous are ordered by Him just like
Psalms 37:23 explains.

I walk through the valley of the shadow of death but I am totally
removed from fear. For the gates of hell can never defeat me as long
as my Lord and Savior is near.

You see he who dwells in His Holy presence is supported by His rod
and staff. His divine protection will always be there for me as I walk
this straight and narrow path.

In the presence of my every enemy He has prepared for me a great feast.
Ironically I share my bread with each of them as
a symbol of a lasting peace.

He anoints my head with oil and my cup continuously overflows.
That's why I'll always lift up my eyes unto the hills and unto
Him uplift my soul.

Surely His goodness and lovingkindness shall follow me for the rest of
my days. And I will dwell in the house of the Lord forever and forever
will I give Him the praise.

OUR MASTER

Bible Study 1

LOVE

Life Overjoyed and Victorious Everyday

Spiritual Reflections:

The greatest gift of all, conceived and established by the supernatural presence of the Most High and the wonder working power of the Holy Spirit. Love supernaturally transforms lives into pure and holy sanctuaries, purposed to glorify the precious name of Jesus.

Scriptural Reflections:

Deuteronomy 6:5
John 3:16
Romans 8:38-39
1 Corinthians 13:8
1 Corinthians 13:13
1 Peter 4:8
Revelation 1:4-6

LIGHT

Luminous Intimacy of God's Holy Trinity

Spiritual Reflections:

That which shatters darkness into extinction. Darkness cannot exist in the presence of light. Our Lord and Savior Jesus Christ is the Light of the world. He alone is the way, the truth, and the light out of the darkness of sin.

Scriptural Reflections:

Psalms 119:105
Isaiah 60:1
John 1:5
John 8:12
1 John 1:5-7

SPIRIT

Sanctuary of Providence and Invulnerability Resurrected to Institute Theocracy

Spiritual Reflections:

God's Holy Trinity is comprised of the Father, Son, and Holy Spirit. The Holy Spirit is the facilitating power of the Word of God. The spirit of a believer in the body of Christ is continually beckoned to yield to the Holy Spirit. Righteous fulfillment in a believer is gloriously achieved when a believer faithfully answers that beckoning call and commences to abide in the word of God righteously.

Scriptural Reflections:

Isaiah 11:2
Matthew 28:19-20
John 3:6
John 4:24
Romans 8:9-11
2 Corinthians 3:17
Galatians 5:25

CROSS

Cost Required to Obliterate Sin and Suffering

Spiritual Reflections:

The figure that is historically and eternally representative of the crucifixion of our Lord and Savior Jesus Christ. Our Lord and Savior committed the exceedingly greatest act of love of all times, when He willingly suffered and died on the cross at Calvary as the propitiation for our sins.

Scriptural Reflections:

Isaiah 53:5
Colossians 2:13-15
1 Peter 2:19-25

BLOOD

Banner of Love Outstretched Over Destiny

Spiritual Reflections:

The Gospel of our Lord and Savior Jesus Christ, the Lamb of God, is the eternal depiction of God's banner of love unto the world. His Blood that was shed on the cross washed away all of our sins and established an everlasting covenant between Him and all that faithfully believe in His Word. There is no greater power in all of creation than the power of His wondrous love.

Scriptural Reflections:

Isaiah 11:10
John 3:16
Hebrews 9:12
1 John 1:7
Revelation 12:11

PURE

Perfected and Upstanding Righteous Existence

Spiritual Reflections:

Faultless in the sight of the Lord, due to abiding in the Lord as His Spirit abides in you. Heeding the Lord's call to salvation and then relentlessly seeking and following His will is the path that a believer must take to reach this pinnacle of righteous fulfillment.

Scriptural Reflections:

Job 1:1
Psalms 24:3-4
James 1:27
Jude 1:24-25

SACRED

Sanctified Article, Cherished Ritually and Established in Declaration

Spiritual Reflections:

A designation that, in the kingdom of God, only the Lord through His sovereignty has the ultimate authority to declare. Whatever He declares as sacred is separated for the sole purpose of dedication to Him. Anything declared as sacred is immediately blessed once it is lifted up to God as an offering.

Scriptural Reflections:

Genesis 2:3
Exodus 3:1-6
John 17:18-19

HALLOWED

Held Above the Land of the Living Omnipotently With Everlasting Dedication

Spiritual Reflections:

A designation that, in the kingdom of God, only the Lord through His sovereignty has the ultimate authority to declare. For example, the name of Jesus Christ is hallowed by God as the Name above all names.

Scriptural Reflections:

Leviticus 22:32-33
Isaiah 5:16
Ezekiel 20:41
Luke 11:2

HOLINESS

Hallelujahs Outpouring unto the Lamb and Intense Noble Enthusiasm Saturating the Sanctuary

Spiritual Reflections:

Exclusive references to the greatest exaltation and dedication in all of heaven and earth, founded on the victory of the precious Lamb of God, and established now and even forevermore. Our Lord and Savior Jesus Christ is the way, the truth, and the light. Verily, He alone is worthy of the sanctitude of holiness.

Scriptural Reflections:

1 Chronicles 16:29
Psalms 29:2
Revelation 4:1-11
Revelation 5:1-14

GLORIFIED

God's Lovingkindness and Omnipotence Reigning, and Invincibly Facilitating the Interdependent Events of Destiny

Spiritual Reflections:

The magnifying of the Lord Jesus Christ on the throne of heaven following His victory over the kingdom of darkness. The Lord is exuberantly proclaimed and gloriously established as King of all kings and Lord of all lords forevermore. Amen.

Scriptural Reflections:

Isaiah 44:23
1 Peter 4:11
Revelation 15:4

HEAVEN

Home Eternally to the Acclaimed and Vindicated Exemplifiers of Nobility

Spiritual Reflections:

The eternal holy city of God where His everlasting dominion of sovereignty resides, and where the Holy One, His angelic hosts, and the redeemed saints of the Lord Jesus Christ dwell. Heaven overflows with the Lord God's exuberance and splendor, and all of those that are there worship Him forever in spirit and in truth.

Scriptural Reflections:

Genesis 28:12
2 Kings 2:1
2 Kings 2:11
Revelation 4:1-2

ANGEL

Abiding Noble Guardian of Eternal Life

Spiritual Reflections:

A celestial being whose thoughts and actions are exclusively set and purposed by God. Angels minister to God, glorify His almighty presence, and serve as the guardians of His eternal kingdom.

Scriptural Reflections:

Psalms 91:11
Luke 1:26-33
Hebrews 1:7

NOTES

HIS MESSAGE

Bible Study 2

SALVATION

Spiritual Alignment to the Lord's Virtues that Admonish Transgressions and Inspire Obedience unto Nobility

Spiritual Reflections:

The sacred spiritual renewal process that the Lord God ordained for the purpose of imparting righteousness into the hearts and souls of His chosen saints and establishing eternal fellowship with them. Salvation is empowered in the name of our Lord and Savior Jesus Christ, and is culminated with the Lord God manifesting to His chosen saints all of His eternal promises.

Scriptural Reflections:

Psalms 37:39
Psalms 71:15
Isaiah 45:8
Isaiah 51:6
Romans 10:1-13
2 Corinthians 6:2
1 Thessalonians 5:8-10

GRACE

Godly Redemption Assured via Christ's Empathy

Spiritual Reflections:

A high dimension of God's faithful love that allows sinners crucial time for redemption from sin by way of salvation and repentance. For all are guilty of sin and have thus fallen short of the glory of God. However, due to His grace, God has established a blessedly assured path to redemption through our Lord and Savior, Jesus Christ.

Scriptural Reflections:

John 1:14
Acts 4:33
Romans 5:15
1 Corinthians 1:4-9

LIFE

Love Incarnated and Forwardly Evolving

Spiritual Reflections:

A heralded gift from God that is divinely perpetuated as a seed within itself. God created man and breathed into him the breath of life. God did this for the ultimate purpose of nurturing eternal fellowship and spreading His love.

Scriptural Reflections:

Genesis 2:7
John 16:21
1 John 5:11-12
Revelation 21:3-4

FAMILY

Fellowship of Abiding Members Interactively Loving You

Spiritual Reflections:

Two or more individuals faithfully consolidated in an uncompromisable bond established through the sharing of compassion, common values, trust, understanding, and common hopes and dreams. A family bond is strengthened when all its members share the love of God with each other and seek His Divine guidance continually through prayer.

Scriptural Reflections:

Genesis 47:11-12
Ruth 1:16
Acts 7:20-21
1 Timothy 5:1

FRIEND

Faithful Relationship Inspirationally Established with Notable Dignity

Spiritual Reflections:

A dependable relationship between two people that forms over time, anchored on trust and on criteria such as mutual feelings and cares, common lifestyles and interests, shared history and experiences, and various interdependencies related to specific needs.

Scriptural Reflections:

1 Samuel 18:1
Proverbs 18:24
John 15:13-15

NEIGHBOR

Nearby Engaging Individual with a Good Heart that Befriends with an Orderly Rapport

Spiritual Reflections:

A friendship initiated and fostered by way of the common proximity of the perspective residences of involved individuals. Though the friendship is established in this manner, it generally continues beyond the period of time that the involved individuals are neighbors.

Scriptural Reflections:

Exodus 20:16
Luke 10:27
Romans 13:9-10

HUMBLE

Having an Unselfish Mind Bound by a Lighthearted Ego

Spiritual Reflections:

A characteristic that is critically essential for shifting attention away from oneself and focusing attention on the Kingdom of God. Having a humble spirit that yields to God serves to promote the Lord's authority in ushering a believer, from glory to glory, unto a righteous life by way of the power and instruction of the Holy Spirit.

Scriptural Reflections:

Psalms 25:9
Psalms 34:2
Proverbs 11:2
Matthew 18:1-5

HELP

Humbly Extending Love and Provisions

Spiritual Reflections:

Administering assistance toward the fulfillment of a recipient's needs and desires. Extending unconditional help is a visible and measurable expression of love.

Scriptural Reflections:

2 Kings 4:1-7
Psalms 121:1-2
Galatians 6:2

HOPE

Help Orchestrated in Prayer and Evangelism

Spiritual Reflections:

Righteous dependence on the Lord for fulfillment of needs and desires. Whenever a believer puts trust in the Lord regarding needs and desires, the faithfulness and lovingkindness of the Lord, in an inspirational atmosphere of hope, serves as blessed assurance to a believer that fulfillment will be met.

Scriptural Reflections:

Psalms 130:5-7
Jeremiah 17:7
1 Peter 1:3-5

TRUST

Total Reliance Uploaded onto the Savior Timelessly

Spiritual Reflections:

Acknowledging the Lord and believing in the power of His Word. Trusting in the Word of God helps to build a firm foundation in the life of a believer and unleashes God's Divine protection against the forces of evil.

Scriptural Reflections:

Psalms 91:2
Psalms 118:8-9
Proverbs 3:5-6
Nahum 1:7
Matthew 6:33

FAITH

Fostering the Anointing Invincibly via Trust and Hope

Spiritual Reflections:

God's uniform, intangible collectiveness of all His eternal resources, and His power that enables its navigation, allocation, and procreation. Faith is the substance of things hope for, the evidence of things not seen. Faith is the building blocks for all that is and all that is to come.

Scriptural Reflections:

Matthew 17:20
Acts 6:8
I Corinthians 16:13
Hebrews 11:1-12

BELIEF

Bond Empowered by the Lord that is Inspirationally Established in Faith

Spiritual Reflections:

The solidifying measure of faith in the word of God that invokes the truth of God inside the hearts of His people. The belief and acknowledgement of God in the name of His only begotten Son Jesus Christ, the Lamb of God, is the birth of spiritual wisdom, the faith unto salvation, and the first steps along the straight and narrow path that leads to eternal life.

Scriptural Reflections:

John 1:12-13
John 20:29
Romans 10:10
Galatians 3:22
2 Thessalonians 2:13-14

NOTES

HIS MINISTRY

Bible Study 3

SAVED

Securely Anchored to the Vine Each Day

Spiritual Reflections:

Salvation immediately ushers a believer into the presence of the Lord. Continuous trust and faith in God leads a believer unto righteousness. The security of a believer is thereby assured, because in His presence is fullness of joy and at His right hand there are pleasures forevermore.

Scriptural Reflections:

Psalms 121:1-8
John 3:17
Romans 10:13
Ephesians 2:8-10

SAFE

Secured Against the Forces of Evil

Spiritual Reflections:

The world defines safety in terms of strength in numbers. In the body of Christ, a believer is safe when safety is dependent on trust in the word of God, salvation in the name of Jesus Christ, and faith in the power of the Holy Spirit.

Scriptural Reflections:

Psalms 91:1-2
Psalms 119:117
Proverbs 18:10

GLORY

God's Love Overflowing and Rising in You

Spiritual Reflections:

The positive life changing impact of the love of the Lord in the lives of His chosen people. The glory of the Lord is the strength unto salvation, the pathway unto righteousness, and the power unto eternal life.

Scriptural Reflections:

Nehemiah 9:5
Psalms 8:1-5
Isaiah 11:10
2 Corinthians 3:7-18

FREE

Fetters Removed and Enemies Eliminated

Spiritual Reflections:

Relief from all burdens by the love of God and the belief in the gospel of His Son. They that believe in Christ are brought out of darkness into the marvelous light and set free from all burdens. Thus, whosoever the Son sets free is truly free.

Scriptural Reflections:

John 8:32
John 8:36
Acts 12:5-10
Acts 16:25-34

FREEDOM

Fetters Removed and Enemies Entirely Destroyed Omnisciently by the Messiah

Spiritual Reflections:

The ultimate harvest from the seeds of God's love facilitated by the power of the Holy Spirit. They that believe in His Son are brought out of darkness into the marvelous light and set free from all burdens. Thus, whosoever the Son sets free is truly free.

Scriptural Reflections:

Psalms 146:7
John 8:32
John 8:36
2 Corinthians 3:17

CALM

Comfort Attained in the Lord's Mercy

Spiritual Reflections:

The result of walking righteously through life filled with the peace of Jesus Christ, the Prince of Peace. Peace is blessed assurance in the Lord's mercy. Because of His peace, a believer can have calmness in the midst of a storm and serenity in the midst of trial and tribulation.

Scriptural Reflections:

2 Chronicles 20:30
Psalms 131.2
Proverbs 17:27
Luke 8:24

COMFORT

Confidence Overflowing Majestically in Faith and Operating Relentlessly in Trust

Spiritual Reflections:

The result of blessed assurance rendered into the life of a believer after personally experiencing the love of Christ and the life changing power of the Holy Spirit. The life of a believer is securely comforted by faith in God and by the perpetuating joy of His Holy Presence.

Scriptural Reflections:

Psalms 23:4
Isaiah 51:3
2 Corinthians 13:11

MERCY

Method of Extending the Righteousness of Christ to You

Spiritual Reflections:

A gift from God divinely perpetuated from His loving grace. Mercy benefits all who believes in Him that they, by the love of God and by faith in our Lord and Savior Jesus Christ, shall come to know abundant truth, and thereby be made righteous by the life changing power of the Holy Spirit.

Scriptural Reflections:

Psalms 100:5
Proverbs 16:6
Jude 1:20-21

JOY

Jubilation of Overwhelming Yield

Spiritual Reflections:

The overflowing endearment and captivating satisfaction rendered into the life of a believer after personally experiencing the love of Christ and the life changing power of the Holy Spirit. The joy of the Lord is strength unto salvation and power unto eternal life.

Scriptural Reflections:

Psalms 16:11
Isaiah 51:3
John 16:24
Hebrews 12:1-2

PEACE

Pleasingly and Enthusiastically Anchored in Christ Evermore

Spiritual Reflections:

The result of blessed assurance rendered into the life of a believer after personally experiencing the love of Christ and the life changing power of the Holy Spirit. The life of a believer that trust in God is blessed with an overflowing fountain of peace that surpasses all understanding.

Scriptural Reflections:

Numbers 6:26
Isaiah 9:6
John 14:27
Philippians 4:6-7

BLESSED

Believers of the Lord Extensively Supplemented and Secure Every Day

Spiritual Reflections:

An abundantly supplemented and secure believer of God's Word. The Lord provides for His people in the form of harvest cultivated from seeds of goodness, such as answers to prayers, rewards for walking upright in the Lord, and blessings that rain down from heaven in response to the praising and worshipping of His Holy Name.

Scriptural Reflections:

Deuteronomy 28:6
Psalms 34:8
Matthew 5:3-11

BLESSING

Bountifulness of the Lord Extended Significantly to the Saved, via Intercession Necessitated by God

Spiritual Reflections:

Bountiful provisions furnished to the people of God for fulfillment of needs and desires, and for pleasures forevermore. The Lord provides to His faithful in the form of harvest cultivated from seeds of goodness, such as answers to prayers, rewards for walking upright in the Lord, and blessings that rain down from heaven in response to the praising and worshipping of His Holy Name.

Scriptural Reflections:

Psalms 24:5
Ezekiel 34:26
Luke 8:43-48

NOTES

HIS MANDATE

Bible Study 4

WORD

Wholehearted Obedience to Righteousness Defined

Spiritual Reflections:

The supernatural cognitive, substantive, and dominative capacities of the Father, Son, and Holy Spirit. The Word of God, incarnated in our Lord and Savior Jesus Christ, is the incorruptible and inspirational truth that invincibly manifests God's eternal love and eternal salvation.

Scriptural Reflections:

Psalms 119:11
Luke 4:32
Luke 11:28
John 1:1-4

LAW

Legitimized Article of the Word

Spiritual Reflections:

A distinct area or element of God's word that is directly implementable into a believer's heart for the purpose of correspondingly thwarting transgressions. In the body of Christ, it is accounted to righteousness on a believer's behalf whenever a believer's love for the Lord inspires heartfelt obedience to God's laws and precepts.

Scriptural Reflections:

Psalms 1:1-2
Romans 3:31
Romans 8:2-4
Galatians 5:14

WILL

Worthy Intercessory Laws of the Lord

Spiritual Reflections:

The makeup of God's eternal plan and events of the Word of God. Through the will of God, the life, death, resurrection, and ascension to heaven of His Son defeats sin. These series of events usher in the restoration of righteous fellowship between God and man by way of His grace and mercy.

Scriptural Reflections:

Isaiah 7:14
Matthew 5:18
Romans 8:27
Romans 12:2
1 John 2:17

TRUTH

Theocratic Revelations that Unmask the Transgressions of Humanity

Spiritual Reflections:

The never changing straight and narrow line of discernment that separates eternal light from eternal darkness. Truth frees the righteous and obliterates deceitfulness. The Lord God is the God of Truth, and will use it to judge the nations on the day of His coming.

Scriptural Reflections:

Deuteronomy 32:4
Psalms 33:4
John 8:32
1 John 3:18-19

BODY

Biological Offspring Devoted to Yearning

Spiritual Reflections:

The physical manifestation of a self-aware, environment dependent life. God is the Creator of all living things, and it is He also that provides the sustenance for all of creation. Those that are redeemed in Him know through faith that the Lord God provides all of their needs according to His riches in glory.

Scriptural Reflections:

Romans 6:12-13
Romans 12:1
Colossians 2:18-19

MIND

Map to the Imagination and Navigator to Decisions

Spiritual Reflections:

The conscience of a person, through which their identity is formed, their life is defined, and their testaments are transpired. A person's mind is the battlefield in the war of good versus evil, and it is where a believer in the body of Christ receives the ultimate victory when choosing to accept the Lord's call to salvation.

Scriptural Reflections:

Isaiah 26:3
Romans 12:2
Romans 12:16
Colossians 3:2

HEART

Habitual Emotions that Administer to Relationships and Trust

Spiritual Reflections:

Habitual sets of emotions resonating in a person during distinct types of circumstances. When invoked, habitual emotions can result in positive and negative ramifications that can affect one's relationships with God, self, and other people. However, those in the body of Christ have hearts that are faithfully filled with the love of the Lord. Salvation results with the Lord creating in a believer a clean heart and a renewed spirit.

Scriptural Reflections:

Deuteronomy 30:6
1 Kings 11:4
Psalms 119:11
Proverbs 15:13-14

SOUL

Sacred Objectives of an Unbridled Life

Spiritual Reflections:

The compositional sets of a life's defining moments. The soul contains the blueprints of all of a person's works in life. A soul of a believer that abides in the Lord contains the blueprints of righteousness.

Scriptural Reflections:

Psalms 23:3
Psalms 86:4
Proverbs 3:19-23
Luke 21:19

REPENT

Regretting Earnestly Previous Events of Negativity and Transgression

Spiritual Reflections:

To truthfully and remorsefully regret sinful thoughts and behaviors, and to subsequently seek atonement with diligence. The pathway to redemption from sin starts with the call to repentance and leads to righteousness, through faith in our Lord and Savior Jesus Christ and the life changing power of the Holy Spirit.

Scriptural Reflections:

Isaiah 55:7
Hosea 14:1-2
Jonah 3:1-10
Luke 11:32
John 1:19-23

VOWS

Voiced Obligations Willfully Stated

Spiritual Reflections:

Honorably beheld verbal exchanges of obligatory words stated before God and man, intended to bind an agreement between one individual and God, or between two or more individuals with God as their primary witness. Broken vows are setbacks to forward progress gained in one's walk with God. However, God's faithfulness is able to instill a believer with renewed righteousness through forgiveness and repentance.

Scriptural Reflections:

Genesis 50:25
Deuteronomy 6:13
John 17:17-18
Hebrews 6:13-20

JUDGEMENT

Jesus's Uncompromisable Decisions on Good and Evil to Mandate the Eternal Nonproliferation of Transgressions

Spiritual Reflections:

A latter day event that the Lord will gloriously complete for the Divine purposes of unveiling His eternally sovereign kingdom and gathering His chosen righteous saints that will live with Him forevermore. The straight and narrow path to righteousness starts with His call to salvation and culminates on and thereafter the day of the Lord's judgement.

Scriptural Reflections:

Psalms 94:14-15
Revelation 14:6-7
Revelation 20:4

JUSTICE

Judgement Upon Sin Theocratically Imposed and Conclusively Enforced

Spiritual Reflections:

The Omnipotent victory in Jesus Christ, who is the Lamb of God and the Lion of Judah. Justice in the Lord is the empowerment of eternal righteousness, and also is the final confirmation to all heaven and earth that Jesus Christ is Lord and King forevermore. Amen.

Scriptural Reflections:

Psalms 37:28
Isaiah 30:18
Isaiah 51:4

NOTES

OUR MINISTRY

Bible Study 5

CHURCH

Consecrated Home of the Uplifted Righteous in Christ, the Head

Spiritual Reflections:

The faithfully redeemed saints of the Lord that will forevermore dwell with Him in righteousness and glory. The Lord is the Head of His church, and gave His life for the salvation of His church. Soon, He will return and receive His church unto Himself, without spot or wrinkle.

Scriptural Reflections:

Psalms 92:13
Psalms 122:1
Acts 2:46-47
1 Corinthians 12:28

PRAYERS

Petitions of the Righteous that Always Yield Everything Requested in Surplus

Spiritual Reflections:

The primary correspondences between a believer or group of believers and God. A model prayer to God consists of a believer acknowledging the sovereignty of God, requesting from God in faith provisions which bolster the lives of those who believe in Him, and wholehearted exalting of the Lord God's eternal supremacy.

Scriptural Reflections:

1 Samuel 1:9-20
Matthew 6:9-13
John 15:7
Romans 8:26-27
James 5:16

CONCERN

Cautious Overflow of Nervousness, Concentrated on Eliminating or Remediating Needs

Spiritual Reflections:

A steady stream of attention given with a heightened sense of urgency towards the hope for positive outcome in the midst of ongoing trials and tribulations. Ineffectively managed concerns become burdens that can weigh heavy on the soul. However, experiencing God's love sets a believer free from all burdens.

Scriptural Reflections:

Psalms 138:8
Matthew 6:25
Matthew 6:34
Philippians 4:6-7

PRAISE

Providence Robustly Acclaimed in Inspirational Singing and Exhortation

Spiritual Reflections:

One or more faithful believers of the Lord God expressing love and gratitude to Him in various forms of intense inspirational celebratory singing, dancing, and exhorting. The Lord is good, and He is worthy to be praised for His goodness.

Scriptural Reflections:

2 Samuel 6:14-15
Psalms 150:1-6
Hebrews 13:15
Revelation 19:5

ARMOR

Adeptness at Repelling the Malevolent Opponents of Righteousness

Spiritual Reflections:

Impenetrable spiritual attire that is fitted by the Holy Spirit inside the hearts and souls of the people of God to effectively defend against attacks from the kingdom of darkness. Spiritual armor consists of truth, peace, righteousness, salvation, faith, and the word of God. Believers must pray continually and bear spiritual armor at all times in order to sustain protection from the kingdom of darkness throughout all tests and trials.

Scriptural Reflections:

Psalms 121:7-8
Romans 13:12
Ephesians 6:10-20
1 Thessalonians 5:8

DIGNITY

Dominion of Integrity, Gallantly Navigating Interpersonal Treatment in You

Spiritual Reflections:

A virtue that empowers interpersonal kindness, respect, and trustworthiness in a person's characteristics and behavior. Treating others with dignity gives credence to a person's integrity, and strengthens their righteousness in the kingdom of God.

Scriptural Reflections:

Genesis 13:5-12
Esther 6:1-9
Proverbs 31:10-31
James 3:18

KIND

Keen Interpersonal Niceness Displayed

Spiritual Reflections:

The act of unselfishly providing help and other forms of positive inspiration for the purpose of uplifting the lives of others. Being kind to others is an effective way of sharing and spreading the love of Jesus.

Scriptural Reflections:

Psalms 119:76
1 Corinthians 13:4-7
Ephesians 4:32

GOOD

God's Omniscience Obediently Demonstrated

Spiritual Reflections:

Everything in heaven and earth, throughout all of eternity, that is attributable in any way to God. God is good at all times, and His mercy endures forever.

Scriptural Reflections:

1 Chronicles 16:34
Luke 18:19
Romans 12:21

DISCIPLE

Dedicated Individual Serving Christians and Inspiring People to Love Everyone

Spiritual Reflections:

A spiritual leader that is wholeheartedly subservient to our Lord and Savior Jesus Christ, and a soldier of faith in the army of the Lord. A disciple leads by example and is anointed by God with spiritual gifts for the purpose of spreading the gospel of Christ all across the world.

Scriptural Reflections:

1 Kings 19:19-21
Luke 6:40
Luke 9:1
Acts 13:52

ADVOCATES

Anyone Dedicated to Voluntary Outreaches of Care that Administer via Testimony, Education, and Supplementation

Spiritual Reflections:

Subservient leaders or followers of worthy causes that manifest increase in the lives of people by way of intercession. Advocates are anointed by God with spiritual gifts to help in the fulfillment of their causes. Our Lord and Savior Jesus Christ is our Divine Advocate, interceding for us in heaven for the cause of our righteousness in Him.

Scriptural Reflections:

Jeremiah 1:7
Matthew 28:19-20
John 14:26
1 John 2:1

CARE

Compassionate Attention to Rightful Entitlements

Spiritual Reflections:

Earnest contributions and prayerful regards given to others for the purpose of resolving needs and advocating quality of life improvements. Caring is a genuine and directly impactful method of spreading the love of Jesus.

Scriptural Reflections:

Psalms 27:10
Proverbs 29:7
Matthew 14:14-21

THANKS

Thoughtful Heralded Appreciation Noted for Kindness and Sacrifice

Spiritual Reflections:

Expressions of gratitude for the previous, current, and future kindhearted thoughts and actions of others. Expressing thanks is an effective way of sharing and spreading the love of Jesus.

Scriptural Reflections:

Psalms 97:12
Psalms 107:8
Matthew 15:36
Colossians 3:17
1 Thessalonians 5:16-18

NOTES

OUR MATURATION

Bible Study 6

PATIENCE

Poised Awaiting of Time to Inspirationally Empower Needs to Come into Existence

Spiritual Reflections:

Holding firm to fortitude and other principles of faith in the midst of adverse situations. A believer's trust in the word of God perpetuates patience and forbearance, thus enabling a believer by faith to triumph over any adversity.

Scriptural Reflections:

Psalms 27:14
Isaiah 40:31
Luke 21:19
Romans 15:4
James 1:2-4

OBEDIENCE

Obligations to the Biblical Execution of Duties that are Integrally Evident of Noteworthy Christian Education

Spiritual Reflections:

The submissiveness of a person or group to guidance and instructions from the Lord God, or from another person or group. Believers in the body of Christ, for example, are submissive to the guidance of the Lord God, and express their exuberance for Him through righteous obedience to His will.

Scriptural Reflections:

Proverbs 3:5-6
2 Corinthians 10:3-6
Philippians 3:12-16

RIGHT

Rewarded Intercession that Garnishes the Hallowed Truth

Spiritual Reflections:

An element of truth that is undeniably sustainable. In the body of Christ, any act that reveals a believer upholding that which is right is accounted to righteousness on the believer's behalf.

Scriptural Reflections:

Psalms 94:15
Proverbs 21:3
Daniel 12:3
Romans 4:3

SEED

Succeeding Evolutionary Element of Destiny

Spiritual Reflections:

An encapsulated miniature variant of a distinct life form source or other distinct source of reference. A seed has the ability to evolve in such a way that can lead to the upgrading, multiplying, or replacing of its respective source. A good example of this in the body of Christ are seeds of faith, which multiple exceedingly, and evolve into eternal salvation and abundant life in our Lord and Savior Jesus Christ.

Scriptural Reflections:

Genesis 1:11-12
Genesis 3:14-15
Genesis 8:22
2 Corinthians 9:10-11
Galatians 3:16

NEEDS

Notable Elements Essential to Daily Survival

Spiritual Reflections:

Requirements for the enrichment and healthy sustaining of a life. A life suffers, deteriorates, and eventually perishes when needs are compromised or otherwise negatively impacted by an oppression-laden society.

Scriptural Reflections:

Psalms 23:1
Matthew 4:4
Philippians 4:19

GIVE

Gratify with Investments Voluntarily Extended

Spiritual Reflections:

A joyful expression of love that is voluntarily transacted whenever one delivers anything of personal value to another. Examples of such giving include rewards, sustenance, acts of goodness and kindness, and seeds of favor. The exceedingly greatest example of giving was done by our Lord and Savior Jesus Christ, when He willingly gave His life on the cross at Calvary as the propitiation for our sins.

Scriptural Reflections:

Luke 6:38
John 3:16
1 Corinthians 12:1-11

GIFT

Gratifying Investment Favorably Transacted

Spiritual Reflections:

An expression of love that has been joyfully and voluntarily transacted by way of one's delivery to another of anything of personal value. Examples of gifts include rewards, sustenance, acts of goodness and kindness, and seeds of favor.

Scriptural Reflections:

Luke 21:1-4
1 Corinthians 12:1-11
James 1:17

FORGIVE

Forgetting and Omission of Retribution on Grievances, and Issuing Vengeance Exoneration

Spiritual Reflections:

Part of the cleansing process for the heart of a believer in situations where trespasses are committed personally against the believer or against the name of God. God has proclaimed that vengeance is His, and He also forgives us of our trespasses as we forgive those that trespass against us. To forgive is illustrative of the grace and mercy that the Lord has given unto us.

Scriptural Reflections:

Psalms 86:5
Matthew 6:14-15
Ephesians 4:32
1 John 1:9

CONFIDENCE

Conducting Obligations Noteworthily with Fulfillment that Illustrates Dedication, Enthusiasm, Nobleness, and Christian Empowerment

Spiritual Reflections:

The result of blessed assurance rendered into the life of a believer after personally experiencing the love of Christ and the life changing power of the Holy Spirit. A believer's trust in God empowers a believer to operate in faith with unrelenting confidence.

Scriptural Reflections:

Psalms 118:8-9
Romans 8:38-39
Hebrews 3:14-15
1 John 3:21

ANOINTING

Ascribed Noteworthy Obedience that Inspires Nature's Transcendence via Intercession Necessitated by God

Spiritual Reflections:

Ability facilitated by God by way of the life changing power of the Holy Spirit to prophetically inspire positive changes on life impacting situations, in accordance to the will of God. Included in the anointing of our Lord Jesus Christ, for example, is the power unto salvation and eternal life.

Scriptural Reflections:

Romans 12:4-8
2 Corinthians 1:21-22
1 John 2:27

HEALED

Having Elements of Affliction Lastingly and Evidentially Defeated

Spiritual Reflections:

Having components of one's life made whole by the elimination of sickness and disease, thus freely allowing the tranquil enjoyments of life to abundantly sooth one's mind, heart, and soul. Our Lord and Savior Jesus Christ died on the cross so that believers in the body of Christ would be made whole through the power of His resurrection.

Scriptural Reflections:

Psalms 103:1-5
Isaiah 53:5
Matthew 21:14
Luke 6:19

HEALING

Help to Eliminate Afflictions Lastingly by the Intercession and Namesake of God

Spiritual Reflections:

The process which ultimately makes all of the components of one's life whole. Healing eliminates sickness and disease, thus freely allowing the tranquil enjoyments of life to abundantly sooth one's mind, heart, and soul. Our Lord and Savior Jesus Christ died on the cross so that believers in the body of Christ would be made whole through the power of His resurrection.

Scriptural Reflections:

Matthew 4:23
Acts 9:33-35
1 Corinthians 12:28
James 5:16

NOTES

OUR MILESTONE

Bible Study 7

HONEST

Holding Onto Nobility and Earnestness via the Sacred Truth

Spiritual Reflections:

A defining quality of a righteous person. An honest person is one who upholds justice, stands faultless before the Lord, and is pleasing in His sight.

Scriptural Reflections:

Psalms 37:23
Proverbs 16:11
Titus 3:8

SINCERE

Saturated Internally in Noticeable Christian Ethics and Righteous to Everyone

Spiritual Reflections:

A common characteristic of people securely anchored in truth and righteousness. A sincere person is one that prioritizes integrity and understands the importance of walking upright in the Lord. In the body of Christ, sincerity is one of the shining lights that lead a believer along the straight and narrow path to Glory.

Scriptural Reflections:

Joshua 24:14-15
Job 1:1
Ephesians 6:24

SACRIFICE

Surrendering All to Creditably Reflect Intense Faith Invested in Christ Eternally

Spiritual Reflections:

A selfless act of love and humility characterized by the faithful willingness of a person to give without consideration of personal need or gain. There is no greater sacrifice than at the cross of Calvary, where our Lord and Savior Jesus Christ willfully died for our sins, so that those who believe in Him would be made righteous in Him through the gift of salvation.

Scriptural Reflections:

Psalms 107:22
Isaiah 53:5
John 19:14-18
Galatians 2:20
Philippians 2:8

PERSEVERANCE

Patience Everyday to Remain Strong, Earnest, and Vigilant in Events that Relentlessly Attempt to Neutralize Christian Empowerment

Spiritual Reflections:

The anchoring power administered to believers by the Holy Spirit to hold steadfast to the things of God while suffering through trials and tribulations. In the body of Christ, victories in perseverance produce praiseworthy increases of faith in the lives of believers, thus furthering the journey of each along the straight and narrow path to eternal life.

Scriptural Reflections:

Romans 5:3-4
Romans 8:25
James 5:11
2 Peter 1:5-7
Revelation 3:10

DREAMS

Destiny's Revelations Entailed in Analyzable Memories as Signs

Spiritual Reflections:

Visual portrayals transpiring in a person's mind outside the scope of reality. Dreams can transpire while a person is asleep or awake, and are generally impromptu. God uses dreams as one of His many supernatural means for inspiring His Word and leading believers down the path towards righteousness.

Scriptural Reflections:

Genesis 41:1-36
Daniel 2:24-45
Matthew 2:13
Matthew 2:19-20

VISION

Vivid Introspective Spiritual Intercession that is Observed Noteworthily

Spiritual Reflections:

When prayers go up, God's blessings come down. One category of such blessings is spiritual guidance by way of wisdom and prophecy. The Lord uses visions as maps to lead His faithful people forward unto closer relationship with Him.

Scriptural Reflections:

Daniel 8:1-27
Habakkuk 2:2 3
Acts 10:1-8

KNOWLEDGE

Keenness in the Necessity of Obedience to the Word of the Lord and Enthusiastic Devotion to Godly Education

Spiritual Reflections:

The seeds of eternal truth and reality in the Kingdom of God. Worldly knowledge dissolves away over time. However, in the body of Christ, believers are relentlessly encouraged in the everlasting knowledge of our Lord and Savior Jesus Christ. They that attain it with due diligence attain eternal righteousness and life in abundance.

Scriptural Reflections:

Proverbs 1:7
Proverbs 9:10
Isaiah 53:11
1 Corinthians 15:34

WISDOM

Willing Indoctrination of Scriptural Dominance Over the Mind

Spiritual Reflections:

The eternally undeniable and never changing thoughts of God, comprised in His Holy Omniscience. The Lord God is the Father of all wisdom and the source of eternal truth. As a believer, following the will of God with urgency results in unlimited access to the wisdom of God.

Scriptural Reflections:

Proverbs 4:7
Ecclesiastes 7:12
Colossians 3:16
James 1:5

VALUE

Vetted Assertion that is Lasting, Undeniable, and Essential

Spiritual Reflections:

A prioritized standard of living that a believer establishes and implements in order to effectively persevere through trials and tribulations, follow dreams and visions, and reach goals and milestones. Having a well-rounded set of values provides a believer with a positive set of principles on which to submit to when having to navigate through the perils of life.

Scriptural Reflections:

Deuteronomy 5:16
Matthew 6:21
Philippians 3:12-14

MORALS

Maturated Obligations to Ritually Accepted Laws and Standards

Spiritual Reflections:

The virtues of God applied willingly and rigorously into the lives of righteous believers over the course of time and generations. Morals are ingrained into the traditions and cultures of righteous societies, families, and people. The souls of those that genuinely love the Lord yearn to express exuberance for Him through adherence to righteous obligations.

Scriptural Reflections:

Romans 12.2
Ephesians 2:10
1 Timothy 4:12

FAVOR

Faithfulness Awarded Vividly Onto the Righteous

Spiritual Reflections:

The Lord avails His goodness and His lovingkindness in abundance to believers that yield to His will and are obedient to His word. He sticks closer than a brother and is always there in times of trouble, for those that call upon His holy name.

Scriptural Reflections:

Genesis 39:1-5
Psalms 5:12
Psalms 91:11-12
Luke 2:52

FAVORED

Faithfulness Awarded Vividly Onto the Righteous Every Day

Spiritual Reflections:

The Lord is not a respecter of person. However, He extends His favor to whosoever that would yield to His will and is obedient to His word. The Lord is faithful and just to those who love Him and worship Him in spirit and in truth.

Scriptural Reflections:

Genesis 19:18-22
Psalms 44:3
Luke 1:28

NOTES

HIS PROMISES MANIFESTED

Bible Study 8

REDEEMED

Released from the Entanglements of Darkness and Evolving Everyday to a Mightily Enriched Destiny

Spiritual Reflections:

Christians that, through faith in our Lord and Savior Jesus Christ, are steadfastly walking the straight and narrow path to eternal life, despite the continual attempts of the adversary to cause as many as he can to go astray and thus miss out on the promises of God. Thanks be to our God that the adversary is completely powerless against whosoever that prayerfully allows the Lord to order his or her steps according to His Word.

Scriptural Reflections:

Exodus 15:13
Nehemiah 1:10
Psalms 107:2-3
Colossians 1:13-14
Titus 2:11-14

RIGHTEOUS

Renowned Individuals that Guard the Hallowed Truth and Exhibit Obedience Unto Sanctification

Spiritual Reflections:

Salvation's elite, that answers the Lord's call and presses forward to utterly overcome, by faith, the sins of the world. The righteous are freed from the fetters of sin through their testimonies of the goodness of the Lord and through their trust in His Holy Word.

Scriptural Reflections:

Psalms 37:25
Isaiah 26:2
1 John 2:29
Revelation 21:7

VIRTUES

Vital Instructions on Righteousness Taught to Unify, Edify, and Sanctify

Spiritual Reflections:

The sets of behavior and character standards that define righteousness. Virtues are the cornerstone of Christian sainthood, and the spiritual adhesive that bonds believers in the body of Christ together.

Scriptural Reflections:

Leviticus 20:8
Proverbs 31:10-12
Philippians 4:8

PROMISE

Provisions of Righteousness Obligated to be Manifested Insurmountably to Salvation's Elite

Spiritual Reflections:

Entitlements that God has faithfully laid up for the righteous in heavenly places. This includes the wealth of the unjust, which is laid up for the just. The promises of God are yes and amen, meaning that they are sure and guaranteed. However, faith is the key. Thus, in order to receive, one must not cease to trust in Him and believe in His word.

Scriptural Reflections:

Genesis 22:15-18
2 Corinthians 1:20
1 John 2:25

SHEPHERD

Savior's Hands Eternally Placed to Hold Everyone that is Redeemed and Delivered

Spiritual Reflections:

An earthly vocation that has many commitments that are relatively comparable to the commitments of our heavenly Lord and Savior Jesus Christ, particularly in regards to His providing for and protecting those that answer His call of salvation. He is the Good Shepherd and we are His sheep.

Scriptural Reflections:

Psalms 23:1
Luke 2:8-11
John 10:11
Acts 20:28

MIRACLE

Monumental and Incredible Result of the Anointing and Consequence of the Lord's Exuberance

Spiritual Reflections:

A supernatural event that transpires in the natural, in total accordance with the will of God. Miracles occur for various purposes, such as the bestowing of blessings, the receiving of signs from God, the invoking of spiritual gifts, and the fulfillment of prophecy.

Scriptural Reflections:

Exodus 14:21-31
Joshua 10:1-15
John 2:1-11

BEAUTY

Bountifully Exquisite Attributes Unveiling a Treasure in You

Spiritual Reflections:

That which is proclaimed to be pleasing to the natural senses, from a respective proclaimer's personal assessment. Supernaturally, beauty is encapsulated in the everlasting Holiness of our Lord and Savior Jesus Christ. He alone is worthy to be praised. He alone is worthy to be worshipped and adored.

Scriptural Reflections:

1 Chronicles 16:29
Psalms 27:4
Psalms 29:2
Isaiah 33:17
1 Peter 3:1-4

HARVEST

Hearty Abundance Received Via Excessive Seed Transformation

Spiritual Reflections:

Abundance cultivated over time from seeds that have been strategically planted and carefully attended to. The seed and harvest concept is resident in all aspects of life. For example, the harvest from seeds of faith is abundant life and eternal salvation in our Lord Jesus Christ.

Scriptural Reflections:

Genesis 8:22
Luke 10:1-2
Galatians 6:7-10
Revelation 14:14-16

NOBLE

Noteworthy Obedient Beneficiary of Life Everlasting

Spiritual Reflections:

A person who abides in the Word of God continually. Through obedience and sacrifice, a noble person overcomes the world and is received in heaven with honor and blessings forevermore.

Scriptural Reflections:

Genesis 5:22-24
Psalms 37:23
1 Timothy 6:12

SAINTS

Salvation's Anointed and Integrated Nobles of a Theocratic Society

Spiritual Reflections:

Those that are the noblest harvest of the Lord, who faithfully exalt the fruits of the spirit above the things of the world. Due to their unwavering obedience to the will of God, they are dedicated with honor and rewarded with eternal blessings in heaven.

Scriptural Reflections:

Psalms 50:5
Proverbs 2:8
Hebrews 10:14

WORSHIP

Wholehearted Overflow of Reverence that Saturates Heaven and Invigorates Praises

Spiritual Reflections:

The acknowledgment and reverencing adoration of God for who He supernaturally is. The Lord is worshipped in spirit because He is Spirit, and in truth because He is the God of Truth. He alone is worthy of worship and praise, due to His perpetual uniqueness and goodness.

Scriptural Reflections:

2 Chronicles 20:18-19
Psalms 99:9
John 4:23-24
Revelation 19:10

NOTES

PSALMS 34 POETIC CONCORDANCE

"I will bless the LORD at all times;
His praise shall continually be in my mouth."

(For praising and worshipping Him is the epitome
of what my life is about.)

"My soul shall make its boast in the LORD;
The humble shall hear of it and be glad."

(All Glory is His, and thus there is no reason to otherwise boast or brag.)

"Oh, magnify the LORD with me, And let us exalt His name together."

(For focusing on the LORD is the only safe passage
through life's stormy weather.)

"I sought the LORD, and He heard me,
And delivered me from all my fears."

(The LORD will not allow for my foot to be moved,
as He protects me all my days, months, and years.)

"They looked to Him and were radiant,
And their faces were not ashamed."

(For the Lord's presence is overwhelmingly awesome,
and there is power in His Holy name.)

"This poor man cried out, and the LORD heard him,
And saved him out of all his troubles."

(Salvation in the LORD is blessed assurance
for persevering through any struggle.)

"The angel of the LORD encamps all around those who fear Him,
And delivers them."

(So let us always give thanks to our precious LORD,
for His lovingkindness is a priceless gem.)

"Oh, taste and see that the LORD is good;
Blessed is the man who trusts in Him!"

(If you eat of His bread and drink of His wine,
never again will hunger or thirst be a whim.)

"Oh, fear the LORD, you His saints!
There is no want to those who fear Him."

(For everyone seeking first the Kingdom of God
will always have the LORD providing for them.)

"The young lions lack and suffer hunger;
But those who seek the LORD shall not lack any good thing."

(For everyone who waits patiently on the LORD
is fulfilled in every way by our Almighty King.)

"Come, you children, listen to me; I will teach you the fear of the LORD."

(For the fear of the LORD is the seed of wisdom,
which harvests into a saint's heavenly reward.)

"Who is the man who desires life,
And loves many days, that he may see good?"

(He is the man with a mansion laid up in heaven for him,
because he follows the LORD'S statutes like he should.)

"Keep your tongue from evil, And your lips from speaking deceit."

(Remember that the Bible verse of Galatians 6:7 teaches us that
what one sows, thus one shall reap.)

"Depart from evil and do good; Seek peace and pursue it."

(And seek to transform your mind to the will of the LORD,
because this is the only way to renew it.)

"The eyes of the LORD are on the righteous,
And His ears are open to their cry."

(All of my days I have never seen the righteous forsaken,
and this is the reason why.)

"The face of the LORD is against those who do evil,
To cut off the remembrance of them from the earth."

(For the ungodly have no inheritance in Him,
and are judged by Him to be of no worth.)

"The righteous cry out, and the LORD hears,
And delivers them out of all their troubles."

(The Lord hears not when the unrighteous cry out,
and thus their lives remain befuddled.)

"The LORD is near to those who have a broken heart,
And saves such as have a contrite spirit."

(Let us praise Him for this in joyful songs that resound
His comforting presence in every lyric.)

"Many are the afflictions of the righteous,
But the LORD delivers him out of them all."

(For the LORD orders the steps of the righteous,
as they faithfully press toward His upward call.)

"He guards all his bones; Not one of them is broken."

(He likewise guards His Holy Word with blessed assurance
on all that He has spoken.)

"Evil shall slay the wicked,
And those who hate the righteous shall be condemned."

(They see their lives as thriving tree branches
before discovering that they are broken limbs.)

"The LORD redeems the soul of His servants,
And none of those who trust in Him shall be condemned."

(Everything that the LORD has promised to His saints
shall be gloriously manifested to them.)

RECESSED IN DIMNESS

Bible Study 9

SAD

Sorrowful, Anguished, and/or Depressed

Spiritual Reflections:

Disturbingly laden with burdensome thoughts, feelings, and/or circumstances. The solution to sadness is joy in our Lord and Savior Jesus Christ. For in His presence is fullness of joy. Sadness is only temporary, but joy is everlasting for the faithful who seek the Lord diligently and are awarded eternal refuge in His heavenly embrace.

Scriptural Reflections:

Psalms 30:4-5
Matthew 11:28
John 16:22
Revelation 21:3-5

TROUBLE

Temporary Repercussions of Outbreaking Unrighteousness that Burden Life's Endeavors

Spiritual Reflections:

The day to day peril and strife in this fallen world. Trouble is a consequence of sin and a catalyst to trial and tribulation. For a believer in the body of Christ, trouble doesn't last always. Steps of perseverance through trial and tribulation build stronger trust and faith in our Lord and Savior Jesus Christ, and are steps along the straight and narrow path to eternal life.

Scriptural Reflections:

Psalms 23:4
John 14:1
2 Thessalonians 1:3-8
1 Peter 5:10

BONDAGE

Burdened, Oppressed, and Needlessly Defenseless Against the Gates of Evil

Spiritual Reflections:

Harassment and other types of oppressive yokes dispatched from the enemies of God, purposed to entrap and ultimately separate people from the love of God. However, through salvation in the name of our Lord and Savior Jesus Christ, yokes are destroyed and those held in bondage are set free.

Scriptural Reflections:

Exodus 6:6
Matthew 11:28
Romans 8:15
Galatians 5:1

SUFFERING

Seeds of Unrighteousness that Form the Fruits of Eventual Retribution, Irrevocably Necessitated by Guilt

Spiritual Reflections:

Temporary torment unleashed onto those in this fallen world for retribution against unrepentant sin, and everlasting torment onto receivers of eternal damnation. Thanks be to the Glory of God that, through salvation in the name of our Lord and Savior Jesus Christ, we have a blessedly assured path to heaven, where suffering will cease forevermore.

Scriptural Reflections:

Genesis 19:24-25
Psalms 11:6
Proverbs 21:15
Romans 8:18

STUBBORNNESS

Selfish Tenacity in Utilizing a Bolstered Bogus Opposition to Righteousness Naively to Nonsensically Elude Submission to Salvation

Spiritual Reflections:

Fierce maintaining of unreasonable contradictions and debates regarding the Lord God Almighty and His incorruptible Word. The adversaries of God reject salvation, and shall therefore suffer eternal damnation. However, the sovereignty of God is everlasting, and all remaining shall bow to His sovereignty and confess of His goodness.

Scriptural Reflections:

Deuteronomy 31:24-27
1 Samuel 15:23-26
Proverbs 26:21
2 Corinthians 10:4-6

ANGER

Animosity Noticeably Garnered and Expressed in a Rampage

Spiritual Reflections:

Divisive outbursts of negativity that are unleashed confrontationally. Anger sparks repercussions that can disparage one's relationships and reputation. However, anger is powerless when confronted by the gifts of salvation in the name of our Lord and Savior Jesus Christ. Love, joy, and peace are among these gifts, with love exalted as the greatest gift of all.

Scriptural Reflections:

Psalms 37:8
Proverbs 15:1
Ecclesiastes 7:9
Ephesians 4:31-32

SIN

Subversive Infestation of Nature

Spiritual Reflections:

Any thoughts, speech, or actions that are contradictory to the word of God or contrary to the will of God. Sin is eternally nonexistent in God and in heaven. However, due to the grace and mercy of God, all guilty of sin have a blessedly assured path to redemption from sin through salvation and repentance in the name of our Lord and Savior, Jesus Christ.

Scriptural Reflections:

Genesis 3:1-19
Psalms 1:1-3
Romans 6:23
1 John 3:5-6

EVIL

Events of Vileness, Idolatry, and Lustfulness

Spiritual Reflections:

Seeds of unrighteousness that contaminate the mind, heart, and soul of a sinner. Evil thoughts and behaviors are like chains and fetters that hold sinners in bondage. However, through salvation in the name of our Lord and Savior Jesus Christ, all chains and fetters are removed and destroyed, and they that were held in bondage are set free.

Scriptural Reflections:

Isaiah 1:16-17
John 3:20
Romans 12:21
3 John 1:11

LIAR

Lawless Individual that Attacks Righteousness

Spiritual Reflections:

One who uses lies to profane righteousness. A liar is an archer whose lies are flaming arrows that target the heart. However, a liar's flaming arrows cannot reach hearts that are solidly protected by the armor of God's Word. Liars use their lies to hold people in bondage. However, our Lord and Savior Jesus Christ is the God of Righteousness, and His Righteousness is the blessedly assured path to eternal freedom from bondage.

Scriptural Reflections:

Exodus 23:1
Proverbs 17:4
Matthew 15:16-19
1 John 2:22

LIES

Lawless Inferences of Evil Sources

Spiritual Reflections:

Deviations from the truth. Lies are flaming arrows that target the heart, but they cannot reach hearts that are solidly protected by the armor of God's Word. The enemies of God use lies to hold people in bondage. However, our Lord and Savior Jesus Christ is the God of Truth, and His Truth blessedly assures eternal freedom from the bondage of lies.

Scriptural Reflections:

Psalms 31:18
Proverbs 14:5
Jeremiah 28:15
1 John 1:6-7

NOTES

RESIDING IN DARKNESS

Bible Study 10

LUST

Lewd Unrighteous Seeds of Transgression

Spiritual Reflections:

Unrighteous thoughts, yearnings, and transpired acts that are aimed at perverting the souls of people and can ultimately lead to eternal damnation. Lust, like other forms of sin, is defeated through salvation and forgiveness in the name of our Lord and Savior Jesus Christ. If we confess our sins to Him, He is faithful and just to forgive us of our sins, and He will cleanse us of all unrighteousness.

Scriptural Reflections:

Proverbs 11:6
Romans 13:14
Galatians 5:16
1 John 2:16-17

ADULTERER

Anyone that Depicts Unfaithfulness by Lustfully Transgressing in an Extramarital Relationship and Evading the Repercussions

Spiritual Reflections:

A spouse that has committed an extramarital act of sexual immorality. All have sinned and have thus fallen short of God's glory. But thanks to the grace and mercy of our Lord and Savior Jesus Christ, an adulterer has a blessedly assured path to redemption and repentance from sin through salvation in His Holy Name. If we confess our sins to Him, He is faithful and just to forgive us of our sins, and He will cleanse us of all unrighteousness.

Scriptural Reflections:

Proverbs 6:32
John 8:3-11
Romans 13:9-10
Hebrews 13:4

LEWDNESS

Lingering Elements of Wickedness Dispatching Nefariousness to Entrap the Soul of a Sinner

Spiritual Reflections:

An evil stronghold that the anointing, empowered through spiritual warfare, is able to annihilate and utterly destroy. Our Lord and Savior Jesus Christ is the Anointed One, and He is also the Light of the world. Lewdness nor any other evil stronghold in the kingdom of darkness can exist in the presence of His marvelous light.

Scriptural Reflections:

Ezekiel 23:35
Romans 13:13
2 Corinthians 12:19-21
1 Peter 4:3

SELFISH

Strivings of an Egocentric Life that Foster Indecency and Scorn in the Heart

Spiritual Reflections:

Placing highest priorities and central focus on personal benefits and wellness. Selfish behavior is a sin that leads to corruption and eternal damnation. However, salvation in the name of our Lord and Savior Jesus Christ transforms a selfish sinner into a faithful believer, who places all trust in the Lord. Those in the body of Christ know with blessed assurance that the Lord God will provide all of their needs according to His riches in glory.

Scriptural Reflections:

1 Corinthians 10:24
Philippians 2:3-4
James 3:16
1 John 3:17

ENVIOUS

Entrenched Nonsensically on the Valuables and Idiosyncrasies of Others, with Undermining Scorn

Spiritual Reflections:

Multiple effects, (evolved from a lack of faith in the goodness of God and a lack of humility), rendering inclinations to yearn after things possessed by others. Salvation in the name of Jesus Christ is the infallible remedy to envy. Those in the body of Christ know by faith not to become envious of others, because they are blessedly assured that the Lord God will provide all of their needs according to riches in glory.

Scriptural Reflections:

Genesis 4:1-8
Proverbs 14:30
Galatians 5:26
James 3:16

GREED

Gathering and Retaining of Everything Essential Demonically

Spiritual Reflections:

Placing highest priorities and central focus on generosity towards egocentric self-interests and personal gains. Greed is a corruptive behavior that is oppressive and detrimental to others. However, by the grace and mercy of God, all guilty of greed have a blessedly assured path to salvation through our Lord and Savior, Jesus Christ. Unless a person guilty of greed accepts the Lord's beckoning calls to salvation and repentance, greed will lead that person on a path toward eternal damnation.

Scriptural Reflections:

Psalms 119:36
Proverbs 1:19
Luke 12:15
Hebrews 13:5

HYPOCRISY

Holding onto Yokes of Pretense that Obnoxiously Convey Religious Imitations of Salvation and its Yearnings

Spiritual Reflections:

Intentional and unintentional pretense to others relating to one's salvation and matters of Christian righteousness. Anyone can be judged by their fruit. However, the only judgement that ultimately matters is that conducted by our Lord and Savior Jesus Christ. Hypocrisy cannot hide from His omniscient judgement. There is no pretense in a believer who truly loves God and relates with everyone with genuine lovingkindness.

Scriptural Reflections:

Proverbs 11:9
Matthew 6:16
Mark 7:6
Luke 6:42

GUILT

Grief from Unrepentant Iniquity, Levying Torment

Spiritual Reflections:

An inevitable outcome of discomfort resulting from any unrepentant act of sin. Guilt is a chastisement from God's righteous judgement that leads to rebellion in the hearts of those that choose to ignore God. Conversely, guilt leads to conviction in the heart of a sinner that is sincerely seeking redemption in the name of our Lord and Savior, Jesus Christ.

Scriptural Reflections:

Psalms 51:14
Proverbs 3:11-12
Ezekiel 18:20-21
Mark 16:16

BIGOTRY

Belligerence and Insults Guided at Outsiders of the Tribal Rudiments in You

Spiritual Reflections:

The mindset of a person that guides hatred towards any group whose respective race, religion, or other traits differ from any of the traits of that person. The adversary uses bigotry in order to separate people from the love of God. However, every attempt ends in total failure. This is because all forms of hatred are eternally nonexistent in God and in heaven. Thus, those that are truly in the body of Christ have the victory over bigotry, and treat everyone with lovingkindness.

Scriptural Reflections:

Esther 3:1-6
Job 8:22
John 4:7-10
Acts 10:34-48

OPPRESSION

Outward Pressures on People or Republics to Extort Submission to Strongholds and Impositions, with Opposition Noneffective

Spiritual Reflections:

Unrighteous authority mandated and maintained through deception and coerced compliance. Oppression is a longstanding weapon in the kingdom of darkness. However, those in the body of Christ know with blessed assurance that all forms of evil are obliterated by the power of the Holy Spirit, and thus no weapon formed against the people of God shall prosper.

Scriptural Reflections:

Psalms 12:5
Proverbs 14:31
Jeremiah 30:18-20
Acts 10:36-38

NOTES

RENDERED IN DESOLATION

Bible Study 11

REVELATION 21:8 NKJV

"But the cowardly, unbelieving, abominable, murderers, sexually immoral, sorcerers, idolaters, and all liars shall have their part in the lake which burns with fire and brimstone, which is the second death."

FILTHINESS

Fostering of Intercommunicative Lewdness, Treatment of Hygiene Impairments with Neglect, and Eluding of Stench in the Soul

Spiritual Reflections:

Having sunken to a condition of life where a final breath of life would lead to eternal damnation. Amazingly, by way of the power of God's love, He can permanently change such a life around for the purpose of His Glory. Nothing is too big for God, and He is not a respecter of person. What He has done in the lives of others, He can do in the life of another.

Scriptural Reflections:

2 Corinthians 7:1
Ephesians 5:5-7
James 1:21
Jude 1:14-18

LAWLESSNESS

Legitimized Articles of the Word Loomingly Excluded in the Soul of a Sinner, Necessitating Either Salvation or Suffering

Spiritual Reflections:

Deliberate noncompliance to the Word of God and disrespectfulness to the Name of Jesus Christ. God has everlasting sovereignty over all things. Therefore, at some point in time and thereafter forevermore, every knee shall bow to His supreme authority and every tongue shall confess of His eternal majesty. The ultimate surrender or defeat of anyone who chooses to oppose the awesome power of the Lord our God is sure and guaranteed.

Scriptural Reflections:

Romans 4:7-8
2 Corinthians 6:14
2 Thessalonians 2:8
1 John 3:4-6

HATE

Hellish Anger and the Terror of Evildoers

Spiritual Reflections:

An evil mindset built on strongholds of anger, vengeance, and deceitfulness. Hate is a primary component in the kingdom of darkness. Conversely, hate is eternally nonexistent in God and in heaven. Salvation and repentance in the name of Jesus Christ is the only solution to hate, because it transforms a person that is on a path to eternal damnation due to hate into a heaven bound believer who treats everyone with love and kindness.

Scriptural Reflections:

Psalms 25:19
Proverbs 26:24-28
John 15:18-19
Galatians 5:19-21

CURSE

Conduct of Unrighteousness Resulting in Suffering and Exclusion

Spiritual Reflections:

Suffering and separation from God, resulting from sin. The death and resurrection of our Lord and Savior Jesus Christ was propitiation for our sin, and rendered for us the grace and mercy of God. Therefore, through salvation and forgiveness in His Holy Name, we now have a blessedly assured path to redemption from the curse of sin. If we confess our sins to Him, He is faithful and just to forgive us of our sins, and He will cleanse us of all unrighteousness.

Scriptural Reflections:

Isaiah 55:7
Ezekiel 18:21
Zechariah 8:13
Acts 8:22-23

CURSED

Conduct of Unrighteousness Resulting in Suffering and Eternal Damnation

Spiritual Reflections:

One that is on the verge of eternal damnation because of a hardened submergence into the depths of sin. The death and resurrection of our Lord and Savior Jesus Christ was propitiation for our sin, and rendered for us the grace and mercy of God. Because of this Holy act of love towards us, there is still time remaining in these final days before His return for all sinners to answer God's beckoning call to salvation, and to correspondingly answer His beckoning call to repentance from sin.

Scriptural Reflections:

Psalms 37:22
Proverbs 10:29-30
Matthew 13:49-50
Romans 6:23

ADVERSARY

Anyone with Demonic Values that is Entrenched on Rejecting Salvation's Atonement and Redemptive Yearnings

Spiritual Reflections:

One who chooses to reject God's love and thus chooses to deny eternal fellowship with Him. Those lost in darkness that do not answer the Lord's beckoning call to come out of darkness and into His marvelous light remain lost forever. This is because darkness is all that an adversary of God can perceive.

Scriptural Reflections:

1 Samuel 2:10
Psalms 38:20
Luke 10:18
1 Peter 5:8

DEMON

Devious Entity Missioned to Oppress the Nations

Spiritual Reflections:

A servant to the ruler of darkness and subordinate in the forces of evil that fruitlessly wage war against the people of God. The people of God achieve victory over the forces of evil by the blood of our Lord and Savior Jesus Christ and by the word of their testimony.

Scriptural Reflections:

Psalms 37:32-36
Matthew 7:15-16
Mark 1:39
Luke 9:1

DEVIL

Devious Entity with Vile Intentions Lurking

Spiritual Reflections:

The ruler of darkness, which is fruitlessly in eternal opposition to the Light of God. God is good while the devil is evil. Evil is an abomination to God, and cannot exist in His presence or in heaven. The saints of God are tempted by the devil. However, they achieve victory over the devil by the blood of our Lord and Savior Jesus Christ and by the word of their testimony.

Scriptural Reflections:

Psalms 34:21
James 4:7
1 John 3:8
Revelation 20:10

DAMNATION

Desolation Afflicted Meticulously upon the Nefarious Adversaries that Trust in Iniquity and Oppose the Noble

Spiritual Reflections:

Forever in isolation, separated from the presence of God and His abundant love. That which is infected by sin dissolves away in the presence of God's Glory, and thus cannot exist near God or in heaven. Eternal damnation is avoidable through salvation and repentance in the name of our Lord and Savior Jesus Christ, which cleanses a believer of all unrighteousness.

Scriptural Reflections:

Proverbs 21:15-16
Matthew 7:13-14
Revelation 20:14-15
Revelation 21:8

HELL

Horrific Eradication Levied upon the Lawless

Spiritual Reflections:

The aftermath of Judgement Day, as those that are accursed, including the devil, are eternally doomed to woeful sufferings. At this point, it is too late to reverse the path or change the consequences of one's evil works. This is because that which is evil dissolves away in the presence of God's Glory, and thus cannot exist near God or in heaven.

Scriptural Reflections:

Psalms 9:17
Isaiah 14:12-20
Mark 3:28-30
Revelation 20:14-15

NOTES

PSALMS 91 POETIC CONCORDANCE

"He who dwells in the secret place of the Most High
Shall abide under the shadow of the Almighty."

(The anchoring protection of the LORD is sure and guaranteed
to anyone that confides in His statutes uprightly.)

"I will say of the LORD, "He is my refuge and my fortress;
My God, in Him I will trust.""

(For the purpose of my tongue is to confess of the LORD;
"All of His ways are righteous and just!")

"Surely He shall deliver you from the snare of the fowler
And from the perilous pestilence."

(The LORD shall give His tender loving care
to those that obey His word without negligence.)

"He shall cover you with His feathers, And under His wings you shall take
refuge; His truth shall be your shield and buckler."

(And within His embrace, the peace of the LORD shall refresh you;
Because you approached Him with salvation as your usher.)

"You shall not be afraid of the terror by night, Nor of the arrow that flies
by day, Nor of the pestilence that walks in darkness,
Nor of the destruction that lays waste at noonday."

(Because you have the victory that comes not through walking by sight, but
by a testament of faith that protects you by God's grace from doomsday.)

"A thousand may fall at your side, And ten thousand at your right hand;
But it shall not come near you."

(Just call on the LORD whenever trouble raises its head;
By faith you know that He will always hear you.)

"Only with your eyes shall you look, And see the reward of the wicked."

(And with your heart shall you remember how your life
was broken before the LORD came along and fixed it.)

"Because you have made the LORD, who is my refuge,
Even the Most High, your dwelling place, No evil shall befall you,
Nor shall any plague come near your dwelling;"

(God's fulfillment of this promise shall not come by power nor by might;
For it is by His Holy Spirit that you are saved and assured of prevailing.)

"For He shall give His angels charge over you,
To keep you in all your ways. In their hands they shall bear you up,
Lest you dash your foot against a stone."

(This is why morning, noon, and night the LORD is worthy of all your praise;
For He sends His angels to guard you and to never leave you alone.)

"You shall tread upon the lion and the cobra,
The young lion and the serpent you shall trample underfoot."

(The LORD is a lamp unto your feet and a light unto your path;
and thus your steps shall never be overlooked.)

"Because he has set his love upon Me, therefore I will deliver him;
I will set him on high, because he has known My name."

(He has surrendered his life to the righteousness of Jesus Christ,
and his faith in the LORD is deserving of heaven's exclaim.)

"He shall call upon Me, and I will answer him; I will be with him in trouble;"

(And I will destroy the evil works of the enemy;
thus bringing end to all scuffles and struggles.)

"I will deliver him and honor him. With long life I will satisfy him,
And show him My salvation."

(And when all has been said and done,
he will be called "blessed" by every tribe, tongue, and nation.)

THE END

ABOUT THIS BOOK

The SOS Spiritual Acronymic Dictionary and Bible Study Guide was written to benefit all of God's chosen people, no matter where one's current place is in the body of Christ. The anchoring focus is aimed at furthering any believer's personal and self-compelling growth in the righteousness of our Lord and Savior Jesus Christ. This is accomplished through prayerfully assembled spiritual acronyms and Bible study content that the reader will discover to be inspirational, entertaining, educational, and edifying.

www.ingramcontent.com/pod-product-compliance
Lightning Source LLC
Chambersburg PA
CBHW071709040426
42446CB00011B/1990